Finance Quest
The Wonders of Money!

Want to step into the World of Finance?

QSHALA
Questions · Quriosity · Quests

Copyright © 2025 by - QShala

All rights reserved.

This book or any portion thereof may not be reproduced or used in any manner whatsoever without
the express written permission of the respective writer of the respective content except for the use of
brief quotations in a book review.

The writer of the respective work holds sole responsibility for the originality of the content and Indie
Press is not responsible in any way whatsoever.

Printed in India

IndiePress

ISBN: 978-93-7197-761-6

First Printing, 2025

Indie Press

A division of Nasadiya Technologies Private Ltd.

Koramangala, Bangalore

Karnataka-560029

http://indiepress.in/

Edited by - Annette Colney, Anagha Sridhar, Bhumika Bagde

Typeset by - Annette Colney, Hakkim Ibrahim

Book Cover designed by - Hakkim Ibrahim

Contents

	Introduction	1
Chapter 1	The History of Money	3
Chapter 2	Needs vs. Wants	9
Chapter 3	Bills and Receipts	13
Chapter 4	Introduction to Banking	18
Chapter 5	The RBI and Digital Payments	24
Chapter 6	E-Commerce	31
Chapter 7	Understanding Investments	36
Chapter 8	Taxes and the Role of Government	42
Chapter 9	Debt and Borrowing Made Simple	49
Chapter 10	Planning for Future Financial Goals	55

Introduction

Why Financial Literacy Matters?

Money is an important part of our daily lives, but have you ever thought about spending it wisely?

Every day, we make decisions about using money, whether it's saving up for something special like a birthday gift or a day out with friends, buying things we need, or even helping others. But being smart with money is not just about having it; it's about learning how to manage it. Many people grow up without learning how to manage money. Without knowing how to manage money, people can end up in debt, overspend, and feel stressed about finances.

When you know how to handle money wisely, it brings both security and freedom. Financial literacy is not just about counting money; it's about making smart choices that can shape your future. So, why not start now?

Here is how it can help you:

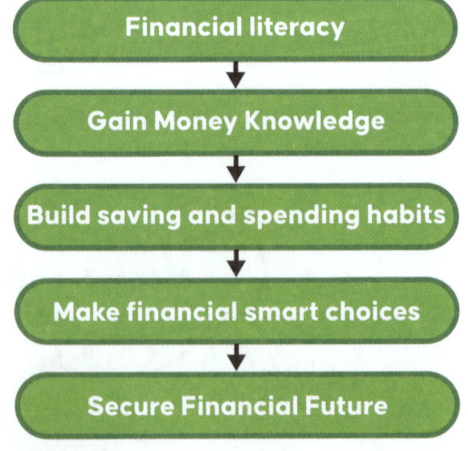

- Financial literacy
- Gain Money Knowledge
- Build saving and spending habits
- Make financial smart choices
- Secure Financial Future

In the chapters ahead, you will join Misha, Ayan, Pia, and Veer as they learn about money. Will they figure out how to spend smartly and save more?

By the end of the summer, money will not be a mystery anymore; it will be their most powerful tool. Get ready to tackle real-life challenges, discover money tips, and test your money skills.

Chapter 1
History of Money

It was an unusual summer afternoon. Instead of the usual bright sunshine, rain poured down, drenching the playground. Ayan, Pia, Veer, and Misha huddled under the big banyan tree in their society, waiting for the downpour to stop. Their usual chatter about video games and movies took a new turn when Pia mentioned how her father was obsessed with Shark Tank.

"Last night, I saw an episode where a teenager started a colourful ice-pop business!" Veer exclaimed. "Imagine making money just by selling popsicles!"

Misha was staring at the raindrops bouncing off the banyan tree's thick branches and said, "I wonder when ice popsicles were first made."

Ayan, always the history buff, leaned forward. "Yeah! And I wonder how much they cost back in Alexander the Great's time. Maybe people even traded them for something else... like salt!"

> **Did You KNOW?**
>
> In ancient Rome, workers were paid a generous portion of salt each day. Over a year, their earnings amounted to roughly 130 pounds of salt. The phrase "worth one's salt" meant a person was skilled and deserved their pay.

Veer burst into laughter. "Salt? That's ridiculous!"

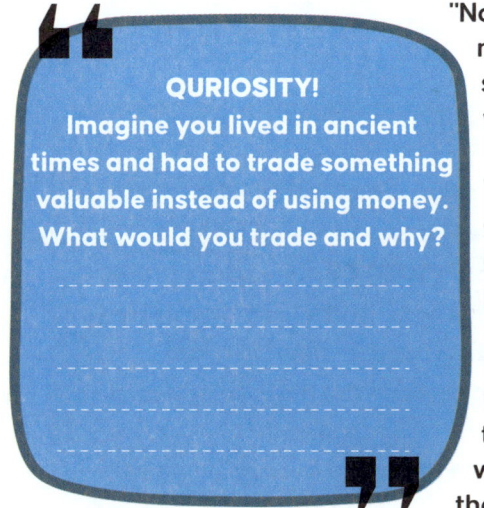

> **QURIOSITY!**
> Imagine you lived in ancient times and had to trade something valuable instead of using money. What would you trade and why?
> ------------------------------
> ------------------------------
> ------------------------------
> ------------------------------

"Not really!" Ayan defended. "My mom once told me that salt was so valuable in ancient times that it was used as currency!"

"So, if salt were still money, we could just grab some from our kitchens and buy unlimited ice pops?" Pia joked.

Just then, a familiar voice interrupted them. "Ah, what an intense discussion!" They turned to see Mrs. Tina, their neighbour, who had also taken shelter under the tree.

She smiled, clearly amused, and continued, "Money has been around for a long time. In ancient times, people used gold and silver coins for trade. But before that, they bartered, exchanging things like salt, grain, or even livestock."

Misha's eyes widened. "Wait... people actually traded goats for stuff?"

> Why do you think the barter system did not survive in the modern world? If the barter system still existed today, how would it affect the way we trade goods and services?
> ------------------------------
> ------------------------------
> ------------------------------

Mrs. Tina chuckled. "Oh yes! As civilizations grew, coins became common, and over the years, they changed in design, material, and value.
Kings and rulers minted their own coins, stamping them with symbols or faces to mark their authority. Later, paper money was introduced, and today, we have digital transactions, credit cards, and online banking."

Ayan's mind was racing. "That means money wasn't always coins and notes. It kept changing!"

QUESTION

Sher Shah Suri ruled the Mughal Empire for seven years after taking control in 1540 CE. One of his biggest changes was in the coinage system. He introduced a new 11-gram silver coin to replace the older mixed-metal coins.
What was this silver coin called, a term which is still used today?

Source: notesonindianhistory.com

The rain had slowed, but their curiosity had only grown. What other strange things had people used as money? And how did we get from trading cows to using credit cards?

As the sun peeked through the clouds, an idea sparked in Ayan's mind. "Guys... what if we try to uncover the coolest, weirdest money stories from history?"

The others exchanged excited glances. "Like a summer mission?" Pia grinned. "Exactly!" Ayan said. "Let's find out how money really works!"

DID YOU KNOW?

Note: Coins were first minted more than 2,000 years ago, crafted by hand using hammers to strike blank metal pieces like gold, silver, or copper.

Earliest Recorded Coins in India

The earliest recorded use of coins in India was 'Punch Marked' coins, issued between the 7th-6th century BC and the 1st century AD.

South Indian coinage featured dynastic crests like the Chalukya boar, Pallava bull, Chola tiger, Chera bow and arrow.

Foreign coins found in India-Ancient India had trade connections with the Middle East, Greece, Rome, and China.

Source: www.rbi.org.in

As Mrs. Tina walked away, the four friends sat in awe, fascinated by everything they had just learned. Who knew money had such an interesting past?
"I have an idea!" Pia exclaimed, her eyes lighting up. "Let's explore the history of money! How cool would it be to dig deeper and learn more?"

Veer, Ayan, and Misha exchanged excited looks and nodded eagerly.

That evening, Ayan couldn't stop thinking about their conversation. Curious to learn more, he asked his father how coins were made. His father told him that modern coins are produced using powerful hydraulic coining machines, which press metal blanks with high force to create detailed designs.

In India, coins are minted at four facilities owned by the Security Printing and Minting Corporation of India Limited (SPMCIL), located in Mumbai, Hyderabad, Kolkata, and Noida. Once minted, these coins are circulated through the Reserve Bank of India (RBI).

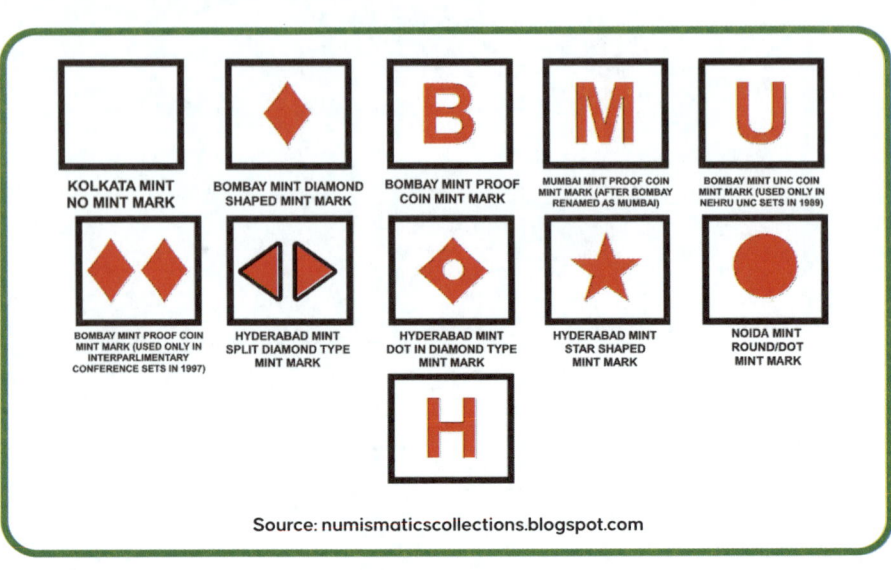

Source: numismaticscollections.blogspot.com

The next day, Ayan could hardly contain his excitement. As soon as he met his friends, he burst out, "Did you guys know that India has four mints that make our coins? And they use huge machines to stamp them with high pressure!"

"Whoa, that sounds awesome!" Veer said. "I always thought coins were just... well, made like that! I think our next mission is to look for coins and check the minting marks."

Which American author and advocate of disability rights features in this special edition coin, making her one of the earliest women to feature on US Currency?

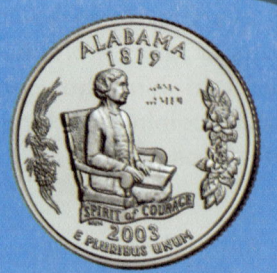

The majestic Zebu bull is found on the seals of an old civilization.
Today, we see this bull associated with which **financial entity, symbolizing power, stability, and growth?**

Just like that, what started as a simple rainy-day conversation had turned into the beginning of an adventure into the fascinating history of money, filled with discoveries and surprises.

Now it's your turn to explore and find out.

Get your detective gear ready!

Explore your home and find some coins. Check the Mint symbol on them and identify where they were made.
Draw the symbol, research the mint facility, and write four sentences describing what you discovered.

Chapter 2
Needs and Wants

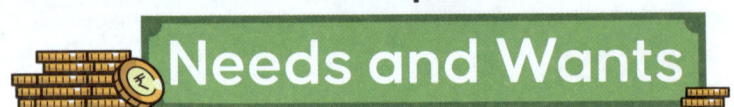

The next day, the four friends gathered under the big banyan tree. It wasn't just any ordinary meeting. It felt like they were explorers on the verge of a great discovery. With their notebooks, pencils, and bags slung over their shoulders, they looked as if they were heading straight into a Jumanji-style adventure!

Pia, always bursting with ideas, flipped open her notebook, its pages neatly divided into "Needs" and "Wants." Tapping her pencil thoughtfully, she declared, "Alright, everyone, let's explore the difference between these two!"

Veer leaned back dramatically. "Easy! Needs are things we can't live without, like food and water. Wants are things we like but don't really need... like video games." He paused, then grinned. "Wait... but I love video games. Maybe that makes them a need for me!"

Pia giggled. "That's actually what I was reading about yesterday! My grandpa told me that in the past, people used to trade rice for jewellery. But what if someone needed rice and only had oil to trade?"

"Great question, Pia!" Ayan said, nodding. "I think that's exactly why money was invented, you know, to make trading easier. Instead of hauling around sacks of rice or salt, people started using coins. Then came paper money, and now we even have digital payments!"

Did You KNOW?

Before money was invented, people had to rely on the barter system, trading goods directly. Imagine trying to swap your comic book for a pair of shoes. But what if the person you were trading with just was not into your comic book? That's the strange thing about barter!

Misha smirked. "But what if someone needed food and wanted jewellery?"

Veer gasped dramatically. "If I lived in ancient times, I'd trade wood for paneer. I love paneer. That's a need, right?"
The group burst into laughter. Ayan quickly jotted down their fun discussion in his notebook. Then, clapping his hands together, he said, "I've got an idea! Let's make a list, some items from the past, some from today and sort them into needs and wants!"
"Challenge accepted!" Pia said, grabbing her pen.

And just like that, their next adventure had begun.

Want to try a similar activity?
  • Look at the BINGO sheet and mark all the items that you feel are necessary for you.

Scenario for you:
A newly discovered planet is ready for exploration, and you have been selected to establish a new civilization there. What five essential items would you choose to take with you?

Clean Water	Internet	Video game	New pair of shoes
A pet dog	OTT Subscription	iPad	A weekend resort stays
Comic Books	Book subscription	Pocket money	A trip to the salon
School Supplies	Bubble tea/ ice cream	A bar of soap	Electric Scooters

Let's test your knowledge

QUESTION

Peasants in the Middle Ages could only afford two items as staples for food along with a serving of soup. Consequently, both items are commonly used as a metaphor for a person's/business' income.
Which two food items are being talked about?

QUESTION

This famous proverb dates back to Aesop's fable "The Crow and the Pitcher" from the mid 6th century BCE. It also appeared in medieval French proverbs alongside "Hunger makes people resourceful," with an illustration of one man eating a carrot and another eating grass.
The Cambridge Dictionary defines it as "If you really need to do something, you'll find a way to do it."
What is the proverb?

Needs

These are the things that you absolutely cannot do without. They are those goods and services that you must have to lead a decent life.
Without these basic necessities, your life may be extremely challenging or downright hard.

Wants

Wants are things that are nice to have but not needed to survive. They can make life more comfortable, fun, or convenient, but they are not essential. Different people may have different wants based on their interests, money, and culture.

QURIOSITY

In the space below create a monthly budget for yourself, what would you spend on needs and what would you spend on wants?
Also explain how would you decide what is more important?

Chapter 3
Bills and Receipts

Veer had the strangest dream. When he woke up, he couldn't stop trying to remember every detail. While brushing his teeth, his mind replayed the dream, under the ancient banyan tree, they had uncovered piles of gold coins! He was bursting to tell his friends all about it.

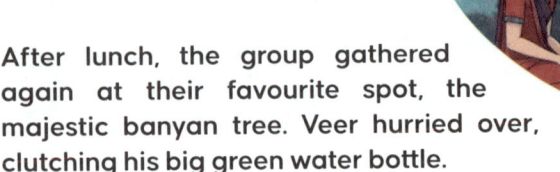

After lunch, the group gathered again at their favourite spot, the majestic banyan tree. Veer hurried over, clutching his big green water bottle.

"There are gold coins under this tree!" he shouted excitedly.

The others paused, puzzled, and turned to look at him.

"Not really, at least, that's what I saw in my dream!" Veer explained. "We dug up the coins and took them to the museum. They even gave us one coin each and issued us receipts!"

"Receipts? Why would they give us receipts, Veer?" asked Pia.

Veer grinned. "I guess it's to prove that the coins were real, like documented proof, you know?"

"I don't think they give receipts for that sort of thing," Ayan remarked, still amused by the idea of museum receipts for gold coins.

The group continued chatting about the old museum in their city until Misha suddenly said. "Hey, I feel hot, how about we grab some ice cream and snacks from the store nearby?" she suggested.

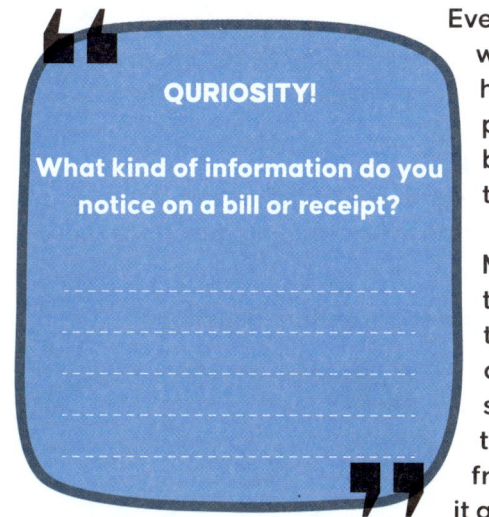

QURIOSITY!

What kind of information do you notice on a bill or receipt?

Everyone agreed, and as they walked, Ayan mentioned he didn't have any money on him. Misha proposed an idea: "Don't worry, I'll buy for all of us, and we can split the cost later!"

Misha held the receipt tightly as the four friends strolled back to the park, savouring their ice cream under the banyan tree. But something strange happened, the paper now looked different from when they had first received it at the departmental store.

"Look at this!" Misha exclaimed, unfolding the crinkled paper. "Veer would say this is exactly the kind of receipt you'd get if you sold something at a museum!"

Ayan squinted at the receipt and chuckled, "Who even sells things in a museum?"

Veer, still half lost in the haze of his strange dream, mumbled, "Us... in my dream."

The group fell silent for a moment, exchanging confused glances before bursting into laughter. Is the receipt mysterious and transformed, or is their imagination at this point. Whatever it was, it added a layer of magic to their day. As they enjoyed their ice cream, they began to wonder if their dreams might be sending them clues to even more extraordinary adventures from all the discussions they have had about the ancient world.

Misha carefully split the bill among the four and mentioned an extra tax section they had to divide. "Imagine if I had lost this receipt, I wouldn't even know how much I'm owed!" she said.

Ayan's eyes lit up as he examined the receipt. "Yesterday, before the cricket match, we ordered pizza on Zomato. Have you noticed that the receipt included a handling charge and a platform fee? It cost us extra!" he exclaimed.

The friends exchanged curious glances. Misha tilted her head thoughtfully. "I wonder what those extra charges are for. Maybe they help cover the cost of running the app or ensure our food gets delivered quickly?"

Intrigued by Ayan's observation, the group decided to turn this into their next mini-adventure. They began brainstorming questions they hoped someone could answer.

You can attempt to answer some of their questions:

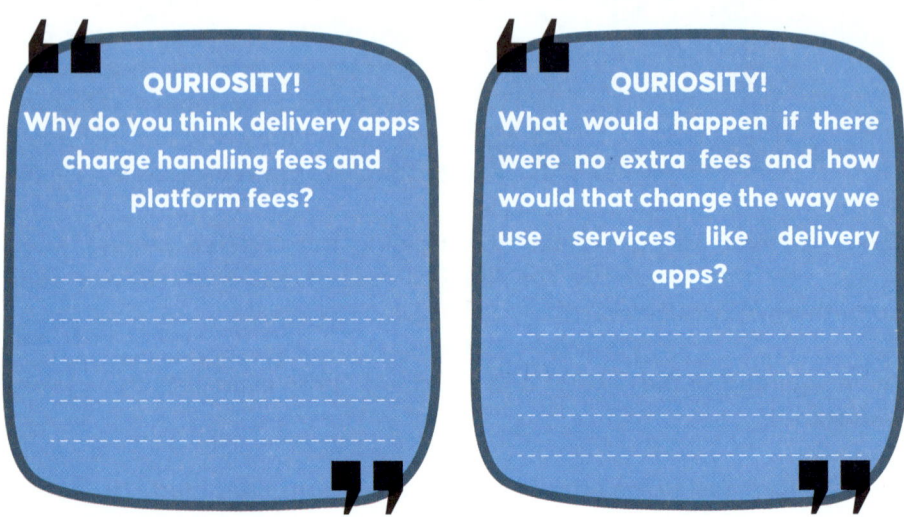

QURIOSITY!
Why do you think delivery apps charge handling fees and platform fees?

QURIOSITY!
What would happen if there were no extra fees and how would that change the way we use services like delivery apps?

Pia nodded in agreement. "Just like our electricity or water bills break down the costs we pay, the pizza receipt reveals hidden fees we often do not notice." With their curiosity sparked, the friends set off to uncover the mysteries behind these charges, ready to explore the fascinating world of modern transactions.

Ayan said, "You know, this reminds me of the bills we get at home. Every bill, whether it's for electricity, internet, or water."

Pia clapped her hands excitedly. "That's so true! And it makes me think about other important documents, like PAN cards and Aadhaar cards. My mother told me that the Income Tax Department issues the PAN card and is essential for tracking our financial transactions for income tax purposes."

Veer nodded eagerly. "And the Aadhaar card? My sister says it's like our digital ID card. Just like our school ID card. It helps us access government services easily and even gets us cool benefits."

Their conversation buzzed with excitement as the friends connected the dots between the mysterious receipt, everyday bills, and essential documents that keep everything in order. It was not just about a magical piece of paper, it was about understanding how every little detail in their lives played a part in a bigger story.

Find an electricity bill from home and look at the details. Then, use your creativity to design your own bill in the space below. Feel free to add fun details and extra sections!

"Maybe our adventure is not just about strange dreams and magic receipts," Ayan mused. "It could be about uncovering the hidden stories behind everything we take for granted from the ice cream we love to the bills and cards that keep our world running!"

With that, the four friends decided to embark on a new quest. They planned to ask questions, learn from their parents, and even visit a local utility office to see how a bill is made. Their journey had transformed into a fun-filled exploration of everyday mysteries, where every document and receipt held secrets waiting to be discovered.

And so, their adventure continued one discovery at a time, filled with wonder, laughter, and a newfound curiosity about the hidden stories in their everyday lives.

Taking a clue of the image identify the phrase related to a warning to be judicious with money?
Identify this financial advice.

Source: www.bbc.co.uk

Identify this financial advice.

Chapter 4

Banking

It was Pia's birthday, and the excitement was in the air. Not only was she thrilled about the party with plans to order food and Boba tea, but she was also eager to introduce her friends to her cousin Leena, who had just returned from an exciting trip to Europe.

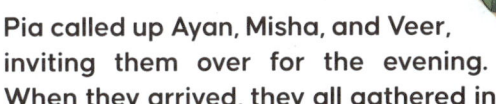

Pia called up Ayan, Misha, and Veer, inviting them over for the evening. When they arrived, they all gathered in the backyard where Leena and her friend were in the middle of a board game. Laughter filled the air as the reunion began.

Pia couldn't wait to hear about Leena's adventures in Europe, especially her visits to captivating museums. Fresh from a two-week college trip, Leena began sharing her experiences.
Veer asked, "I want to go on a long trip too, but it seems so expensive I'm not sure I'll ever have enough money."
Ayan and Misha agreed, adding that they would never have a huge sum for travel.

Leena smiled. "I didn't start with a lot of money either." When I was in school, I used to save my pocket money in a piggy bank, but I always ended up spending it. Later, I started saving in a bright embroidered purse my aunt had brought me from her visit to Jaipur–but I still kept spending. It felt like the more I saved, the more I wanted to spend. Then my dad told me about banks, where I could deposit my pocket money and keep it safe. Many banks even offer savings accounts for students.

When you deposit money in a bank, it stays safe, and you even earn a little extra called interest. I opened a savings account at BDCI Bank, and that's how I funded my trips!"

Misha looked curious. "Interest?"

Leena explained, "Think of it as a reward for saving. The bank uses the money you deposit to lend to others, and in return, it pays you a small amount as interest. Over time, your savings grow."

Ayan's face lit up. "That sounds cool! So instead of keeping money at home, I could save it in a real bank and watch it grow?"

QUESTION

A device was installed at a Shillong hospital in 2021. This was apt considering that the British inventor seen here was born at this hospital in 1925.

Which self-service equipment, first operationalized by Barclays in 1967 at their Enfield, North London branch, is being talked about?

Source: www.theguardian.com

"Exactly!" Leena said. "Banks do much more than just store money. They help people buy homes, start businesses, and even pay for college through loans."

Veer's eyes widened. "Wow! I didn't know we could have bank accounts of our own!"

Inspired by Leena's story, the friends began dreaming about the adventures they could have if they saved smartly.

Pia asked, "Can you tell us how you opened your account, Leena Akka?"

"Of course!" replied Leena, seeming excited about it.

What would you need to open a bank account?
- Any government issued document that establishes your date of birth
- Know Your Customer (KYC) of your parents/guardians:
- Identity proof: to establish their name and date of birth
- Address proof: to establish their residence

Note: A bank usually has branches across several locations. Every branch is identified with an 11-digit code called IFSC (Indian Financial System Code)

QUESTION

Shown here is smart sip tender coconut that informs the user of the volume of coconut water, sweetness level of the water.

Hence, this innovation is a pun on which identity verification process followed by banks to assess the risk?

Source: thecurius.wordpress.com

Imagine planning an exciting trip with your friends.
- Draft a simple budget showing how you will save money regularly and what you will spend it on.
- Also note what expenses (transportation, food, lodging, activities, etc.) do you expect?

> The ATM Machines of a private bank are named after the plant pictured here. Which bank, started this service in 2004?

Leena continued, "At one museum, I learned that in early civilizations, temples were considered the safest places to store valuables. Their strong, always-guarded structures kept thieves away. In Egypt and Mesopotamia, people deposited their gold in temples for safekeeping."

Did You KNOW?

By the 18th century BC, records show that temple priests started making loans with that gold. And just like that, the concept of banking was born!"

She added, "By the 4th century BC, Greek banking had become really advanced. Private businessmen, temples, and government organizations all ran banks. They accepted deposits, gave loans, exchanged coins, and checked coins for weight and purity. They even kept detailed records. Some moneylenders could make a payment in one city and give you credit in another, so you didn't have to carry a lot of coins around."

The friends listened in awe as Leena explained how these ancient practices laid the groundwork for modern banking.
With every story, their eyes sparkled with wonder, realizing that the journey of money from ancient temples to modern banks was as fascinating as any adventure they could imagine.

> India is a cash economy. So, shopkeepers tend to give candy when there's a shortfall, which often means customers losing one, two, five or even ten bucks.
> Hence, which brand, launched another candy - Sweet Change - allowing customers to redeem for actual currency?

Shown here is a font called Farrington B, created by David H. Shepard, the inventor of a certain technology. Gasoline pump stations were among the earliest adopters of this innovation.

The simple, boxy font was designed to minimize smearing from grease, oil, and other substances. Hence, it became the standard for a range of products that are seen everywhere. On which products is this font most commonly used?

```
ABCDEFGHIJKLMNOPQRSTUVWXYZ♪♀H|
abcdefghijklmnopqrstuvwxyz■•¬:¦=
0123456789+/*"{}%?&'-$∧〖〗<>
()!#@\ÜÑÄØÖÆ£¥
```

Leena showed them pictures from her phone. She continued, "There is a remarkable collection of early cheques dated from 1660–65. That was when cheques emerged as a way to transfer money without the need to carry heavy coins or cash," Leena said.
Ayan chimed in, "Like the cheque paper we have now?"

Which financial institution's logo is inspired by these double-mohur coins? It was chosen to symbolize India's economic history and legacy.

Source: en.numista.com

The earliest known cheque, drawn by Clayton and Morris in 1659, is part of a collection that also features the first Harry Potter poster illustration. Which British-founded multinational corporation is associated with this collection?

"Exactly! When I had a part-time job, I got paid by cheque, and I had to go deposit it at the bank. But trust me, those old cheques looked nothing like what we see now, they were like little pieces of history!"

The friends leaned in, fascinated by the glimpse into a time when something as simple as a cheque transformed the way people handled money.

Leena's friend Kriti continued, "Cheques started a long time back. In the 17th century, people began writing orders now known as cheques that instructed banks to pay a specific amount to someone else."

"Take a look at the first look of the cheque drawn of Clayton and Morris in the year 1659." said Misha pointing at the phone.

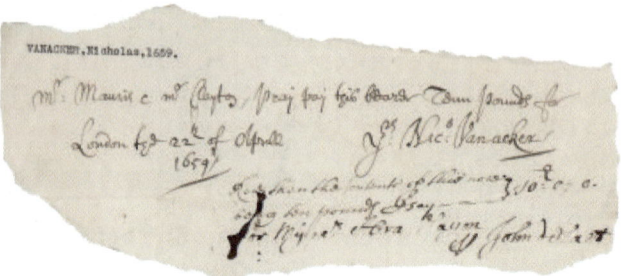

Source: www.sothebys.com

QURIOSITY

What made people trust temples with their valuables in ancient times, and how do these security measures compare to the ways we protect our money today?

Chapter 5
RBI and digital payments

Ayan, Pia, Misha, and Veer could not stop thinking about their eye-opening chat with Leena. Her words had sparked something, a mix of excitement and many questions. They were pumped about the idea of saving money, but one big step was standing in their way: opening a bank account.

"We have to start somewhere," Pia said, tapping her pencil against her notebook. "We can't just keep stuffing coins into jars forever!"

Misha's eyes lit up. "What if we open an account at QFLB Bank like Leena? She already figured it out and it worked for her, right?"
"Let's do it," Ayan said, eyes gleaming. "It's time to take this financial mission to the next level!"
Pia chimed in and said, "I spoke to Ma yesterday about opening an account and we might go to the bank this weekend. I'm excited and I think it's the perfect time to start saving."

Veer frowned, a hint of worry in his eyes. "I read about an elderly person losing lakhs from his savings account. What if we put our money in the bank and they lose it? Who makes sure the banks follow the rules?"

Hearing this, Misha stepped in. "Oh yes! I remember a similar case like that. I think he had mistakenly called a fraudulent number that was posing as the head of the bank."

Leena who was also with them replied, "That was unfortunate, and it is important to be aware of such scams and take necessary actions."

"Shouldn't the Reserve Bank of India look at all these cases?" asked Veer.

Everyone looked at Leena who replied, "See, with the rise in digital payments and the advancements of technology scammers are using different techniques. The RBI being the central bank and regulatory authority has been educating people about staying safe. It is responsible for overseeing India's banking system and currency. However, it is also important for us to be cautious at all times."

> In late 2019, a staff test error caused the United States Department of Agriculture to mistakenly list this fictional, vibranium rich country as a 'former free trade partner' for trading goods like ducks, donkeys, and dairy cows.
> Which fictional country was added to the list?

It's like the boss of all banks in India, making sure everything runs smoothly and fairly."

Ayan's eyes lit up with curiosity. "So, the RBI is like a watchdog for banks?"

"Exactly!" Leena nodded. "It sets rules that banks must follow through measures like licensing, supervision, and conducting inspections and audits. It also serves as the regulatory authority, issuing guidelines. If a bank runs into trouble, the RBI can step in to help. That's why it's called the 'lender of last resort'."

> 'Money Kumar' is a comic-book that is published to teach financial awareness to children.
> Which financial organization that was set-up in India in on 1st April 1935 publishes this comic books?

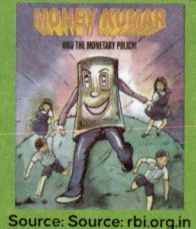

Source: Source: rbi.org.in

Pia asked, "Lender of last resort? What is that?"

"It means if any bank runs into a problem and requires help with financial difficulty, the RBI helps out by giving them the loan they require," explained Leena.

Misha leaned forward. "Wait, does the RBI just sit there and make rules for banks?"

Leena laughed. "Oh, it does a lot more!
You know the money we use every day? The RBI prints it! Every note you have in your wallet, from ₹10 to ₹2000, is issued by the RBI." She took out a ₹500 note and pointed to a line. "See? It says 'The Reserve Bank of India.'

Did You KNOW?

The RBI prints all banknotes in India, except for ₹1 notes, which are printed by the Government of India.

That's proof that the money is real."

Leena continued, "The RBI also controls inflation, it makes sure that prices don't rise too fast. Imagine if a biscuit packet that costs ₹20 today suddenly cost three times more next month. That would make it really hard for people to afford basic things like food and transport."

Ayan scratched his head. "But how does it do that?"

"The RBI controls interest rates," Leena explained. "If it raises interest rates, banks charge more for loans, and people borrow less money. That slows down spending and keeps prices from rising too quickly. And if the economy needs a boost, the RBI can lower interest rates, making it easier for people to borrow and spend."

QUESTION

Source:therbimusuem.org

RBI museum in Kolkata offers various avenues to understand the institution. One is through a game - Mokshapat, is the older name of this ancient game. It was based on morality lesson that a person can attain salvation by doing good. Whereas by doing evil, one will be reborn to lower forms of life.
Which game?

Misha grinned. "Okay, so the RBI is like the manager of India's money, making sure banks are fair, printing cash, and keeping prices under control."

"Exactly," Leena said. "It also helps when companies in India do business with other countries. The RBI keeps a check on how much foreign money is coming in and handles the exchange of money between different currencies. If it didn't do this, the value of the rupee could keep changing a lot, making buying and selling things from other countries confusing and risky."

QUESTION

India imports nearly two-thirds of its annual consumption of a particular commodity. When the price for this commodity drops it is generally good for the Indian economy as it lowers inflation rates and trade deficits with other countries. Which commodity, whose largest exporters are shown in this map?

Source: howmuch.net

Leena said, "It ensures and regulates that foreign money transactions happen fairly. It even helps decide how much of a country's money should be kept in foreign reserves."

Ayan thought for a moment and then asked, "Does the RBI help people directly, like how banks give loans?"

"Not exactly," Leena replied. "The RBI doesn't give loans to regular people like us, but it does lend money to banks when they need it. It also keeps an eye on digital payments, making sure apps like UPI, Google Pay, and payment platforms work safely and securely.

Did You KNOW?

The RBI Staff College in Chennai, established in 1963, offers training and education to RBI officers and central bankers from India and abroad. The campus has a library, computer centre, a gymnasium, and swimming pool for participants.

It helps prevent fraud and ensures that your online transactions are protected."

QUESTION

The Reserve Bank of India Museum in Kolkata has a section dedicated to American inventor Linus Yale Jr.

Shown here is an earlier version of one of his contraptions, widely used in banks and households across the world.
What was his contribution?

The four of them continued asking Leena about the safety of digital payments.

"So, how does UPI actually work?" Veer asked, curious.

Leena smiled. "UPI, or Unified Payments Interface, is like a bridge that connects different bank accounts in one place. It allows instant money transfers using just a mobile number or UPI ID, without needing account details every time."

Misha raised an eyebrow. "But how is it safer than using a debit card?"

"Good question!" Leena replied. "UPI uses multi-layered security, like PIN authentication and encryption, to keep transactions safe. Plus, banks and the RBI monitor it closely to prevent fraud."

Ayan nodded. "And that's why we should never share our UPI PIN with anyone."

In this country the NPCI International Payments Limited (NIPL), in partnership with Lyra, enabled the acceptance of the Unified Payments Interface (UPI) for Indian tourists to book tickets online for a famous landmark. Which country?

"Exactly!" Leena said. "Scammers often trick people into sharing their PIN or clicking fake payment links. Always double-check before making any transaction."

Pia thought for a moment. "I heard about something called UPI AutoPay. What is that?"

Leena explained, "UPI AutoPay is for recurring payments, like subscriptions or EMI payments. Instead of manually paying every time, you set it up once, and it happens automatically!"

"That's actually pretty cool," Veer said. "Digital payments have really changed the way we handle money."

"Definitely," Leena agreed. "And with features like real-time tracking, refunds, and security measures, it's only going to get better."

The group nodded, feeling more confident about using UPI and digital payments wisely.

Veer shook his head. "I never knew there was such a big system managing it behind the scenes."

> The Centre for Advanced Financial Research and Learning (CAFRAL) studies key topics related to India's economy, such as inflation, growth, government spending, foreign trade, financial markets, and monetary policy. Which organization does this research wing belong to?
>
> ---------------------------------

Leena smiled. "Well, you can trust that your money is safe, your bank follows the rules, and your savings will still be valuable in the future."

> Atul S Pande is a Pune-based graphic designer who works primarily on logo design. He is best known for his entry into a 2010 design competition, which featured half a sun surrounding a fingerprint. What design, whose early sketches are shown here, is he best known for?
>
> ---------------------------------

Misha, looking at the others said. "This makes me feel a lot better about opening a bank account! Maybe one day, with our savings, we can even go on that dream trip together."

QURIOSITY

What do you think would happen if our country could print unlimited money without any planning?

Chapter 6
E-Commerce

A week had passed since the birthday party, and the days were getting warmer. The group was hanging out outside Ayan's house when Veer strolled in, flipping the brim of his brand-new reversible cap with vibrant dual colour.

"Whoa, that's awesome!" Misha said, reaching out to feel the fabric. "Where did you get this?"

Veer grinned, adjusting the cap. "Found it online! I think it's from a small retailer. I'd never heard of this brand before, and neither had my sister. But it had 4.8 stars, tons of good reviews, and the best part? I used a promo code and got a discount!"

"Did you compare the prices? The prices may vary even for the same items across different platforms," asked Ayan.

Veer took out his cap and replied, "Of course, I did, people!

Ayan's eyes lit up. "Hmmm... how do these small retailers even manage to sell on these platforms? It must take a huge team with logistics, packaging, tracking orders and it all sounds so complex!"

Veer said, "Luckily, this platform made the process super smooth, and it arrived right on time. But imagine everything happening behind the scenes like tracking payments, ensuring deliveries happen on schedule."

> With the rise of e-commerce and digitalization, ensuring safe transactions and customer protection is crucial for attracting and retaining customers.
> How is this maintained by e-commerce platforms?
>
> ---------------------------------

Misha nodded. "Yeah, with E-commerce, buying and selling online has completely changed how we shop. Businesses don't even need a physical store anymore, just a good website and a platform to reach customers."

Ayan added, "E-commerce has exploded in the last decade! Think about it. Before, we had to go to a store to buy something. Now, we can shop from anywhere, anytime. And these platforms handle everything like warehousing, delivery, even returns."

Pia nodded. "You know what worries me the most? Payments. I could never bring myself to buy something really expensive on these platforms. What if the money doesn't go through and gets stuck somewhere?"

Veer looked puzzled. "Where would it even get stuck, though?"

Pia frowned, thinking of a worst-case scenario. "Imagine placing a big order, and just as you're paying, the app crashes. Your money is debited, but the store never receives it, and you cannot contact the customer care. That would be a nightmare!"

Ayan shrugged. "I think there's a refund process for situations like that. The money usually bounces back in two or three days."

"But I'd still be so stressed during that time," Pia muttered.

> **Famous for its iconic Siren logo and social media buzz, this coffee chain introduced compostable cups with moulded fibre and bioplastic liners. Despite mixed reviews, it aims to make all its cups 100% compostable, recyclable, or reusable by 2030. Which company is this?**
>
> ------------------------------

She hesitated for a moment, then added, "Also, maybe I'm just skeptical, but those pop-up ads always seem sketchy. Like, 'FLASH SALE! OFFER! LIMITED TIME OFFER!' That stuff freaks me out"

> Initially launched as a gift personalization platform and later acquired by Flipkart, this e-commerce giant was among the first in India to introduce the "Try & Buy" option. Now, it has entered the quick commerce race, offering 30-minute fashion delivery for its range of items. Which platform is this?
>
> ----------------------------------

Misha spoke about how she remembered reading about smart online shopping, with a highlighted text that said "Not every 'great deal' is actually great."

QUESTION

This is a cybercrime in which a person is contacted by email, telephone or text message by someone posing as a legitimate institution to trick them into providing personal information, banking & credit card details, and passwords. Which cybercrime, that might remind you of a common profession?

Ayan grinned. "Which is exactly why you should only trust secure websites with trusted payment gateways to avoid online scams and fraud. And yeah, just be mindful about what you share, like your OTP or bank details online, that's just asking for trouble."

"Curiosity has kicked in. Let's do a quick search on how online shopping actually works," Pia suggested, pulling out her phone. "I mean, how do these platforms even manage so many sellers, payments, and deliveries to different regions all at once?"

Misha nodded eagerly. "Yeah! We buy things online, but we don't really think about the BTS. Speaking of BTS, gosh I like their new song!"

> Founded in 1994 as an online bookstore, this company introduced the concept of online book reviews, allowing readers to share their opinions. It quickly expanded to selling CDs, DVDs, and more. Today, it's one of the biggest e-commerce platforms, offering everything from food to furniture. Which store?
>
> ------------------------------

Ayan typed "How do e-commerce platforms work?" into the search bar, and within seconds, a list of results popped up. "Look at this," Ayan said, scrolling and reading. "Okay, so, E-commerce connects buyers to sellers, who can be big brands or small businesses." Most e-commerce platforms use something called a payment gateway. It checks if the payment is secure before sending it to the seller. If something goes wrong, the money gets refunded."

Pia still looked unconvinced. "And what about fake sellers? What about people who take money and never deliver anything?"

Ayan added, "Platforms have seller verification. They check businesses before letting them sell. Plus, they have return policies, customer reviews, and ratings so people can see if a seller is trustworthy."

Veer nodded. "That's why I checked the reviews before buying my cap. If a seller has tons of good reviews, they're probably reliable."

Ayan continued, "It's fascinating how online shopping is growing so fast. Just imagine, guys, we can get groceries, gadgets, even medicines delivered to our doorstep. If people from ancient times could time-travel and see all this, they'd be completely mind-boggled!"

> In October 2022, as part of a 'reverse shopping' campaign shops of a certain company in 3 Belgium cities (Evere, Namur and Ghent) have changed their name to 'Nohltaced' for one month. Which company? What was the objective of the campaign?
>
> ------------------------------

"Yeah," Veer said. "With 'quick commerce,' we can get things in just 10 to 30 minutes!"

Pia giggled. "My indecisiveness could never! I can barely decide what to order in that time."

They all laughed.
"But you know," Pia continued, "with all this convenience, it's important to shop smart. Always check seller ratings, use secure payment options, and cross check deals that seem too good to be true."

Veer gave a thumbs-up. "Good call! I have read and heard about such bad experiences. Its best to be cautious. Let's shop smart and not fall for shady discounts."

Misha chuckled. "Alright then, e-commerce experts, who's up for some real-world shopping this weekend at Orion Mall with Leena?"

The group laughed, feeling a little wiser about the world of e-commerce and maybe just a bit more confident about their next online purchase.

Explore different delivery methods and their logistics! After your research, imagine launching your own online business with a unique delivery system. What would it be, and how would you ensure its success?

Chapter 7
Understanding Investments

Veer's mother had made delicious chikoo ice cream, and Veer had invited his friends over to enjoy it. But what excited them even more was the latest FIFA PS5 game that Veer had just bought!

As Pia and Veer started playing, Ayan watched them closely. The realistic graphics, the intense gameplay, all looked incredible. The more he watched, the more he wanted a PS5 for himself.

"Who got this PS5 for you, Veer?" Ayan asked, still glued to the screen.

"I bought it from Croma," Veer replied, expertly dodging a defender in the game.

"This is so cool! I want one too, but it's way too expensive," Ayan sighed.

Veer nodded. "Yeah, I had to save up for months. But why don't you wait for the Black Friday Sale? The discounts are pretty good then."

"Oh yeah! That discounts are pretty good during that time," Misha said.

That night, Ayan couldn't stop thinking about the PS5. He had some money, but not enough.

The next day, his sister, Sanvi was heading to the mall with her friend. Ayan decided to join them instead. While at the mall with his sister and her friend, the gadget store caught his attention. Sanvi and her friend were talking about the new movie about Stock market they had seen recently. Ayan tried to be part of the conversation, but he could not follow up.

Just then they passed the gadgets section. Rows of shiny new gaming consoles and accessories were displayed behind the glass. His focus had shifted from their conversation to the items displayed.

He walked closer, staring at the price tag of the PS5.

Still too expensive.

> **The Stock Exchange is a book written by a fund manager Ajit Dayal in 1988. To make it more relatable, he collaborated with Vasant Halbe, an illustrator known for his work in a widely popular children's magazine filled with engaging comics and stories. This added a visual appeal to the book. Which children's magazine is Vasant Halbe most closely associated?**

After their trip to the mall, Ayan and his sister, Sanvi, returned home. She noticed him deep in thought.

"What's on your mind, Ayan? Did you want to buy something?" Sanvi asked.

Ayan sighed. "I really want a PS5, but it's so expensive. Veer said I should wait for the Black Friday Sale, but even with discounts, I don't think I'll have enough."

Sanvi nodded. "That's a smart plan. It's good to wait for a sale. But you do have some money saved up, right? I remember you asking Papa to deposit your savings in the bank account you recently opened. Have you ever thought about investing your money instead?"

Ayan frowned. "Investing? I thought that was only for working people."

Sanvi chuckled. "Not really! Not at all! The earlier you start, the better. Your money can grow on its own if you invest smartly. Investing just means putting your money into something that grows over time. You know how you keep your savings in a piggy bank? What if instead, you put them in a Fixed Deposit (FD) at the bank?"

Sanvi pulls out her tab and shows a graph of how money grows over time.

The term "_____ investor" originally referred to wealthy individuals who provided financial backing for Broadway shows.
Professor William Wetzel, founder of the Center for Venture Research, is credited with coining the phrase. He published a study about early-stage investing back in 1978.
Fill in the blank.

"See this? If you put ₹1000 in a savings account, it stays ₹1000. But if you invest in mutual funds or stocks, it can grow over time."

Ayan's curiosity grew. "What's a Fixed Deposit?"

"It's like levelling up your money!" Sanvi explained. "If you keep your savings at home, it just sits there. But in an FD, the bank adds extra money called interest to what you save. The longer you keep it, the more it grows!"

Designed in 1971 by graphic design student Carolyn Davidson for just $35, the iconic logo initially failed to impress the company's founder, Phil Knight.
As a gesture of appreciation, Davidson was later given an envelope containing an undisclosed amount of stock in the company.
Which company, originally known as Blue Ribbon Sports and famous for its celebrity endorsement deals with top athletes, is this?

Ayan's eyes widened. "So, if I put my money in an FD, it earns money for me?"

"Exactly!" Sanvi smiled. "It's a safe and smart way to grow your savings."

Ayan thought for a moment. "So... instead of just waiting for my allowance, I can make my savings work for me?"

"Yes! And if you invest early, by the time the Black Friday Sale comes, you might have more than enough for your PS5!"

Sanvi explained different investing options in India. "There are so many ways to invest! You can try:"

Mutual Funds (SIP) – "Think of it like planting a small tree. You put in a little money regularly, and over time, it grows into something bigger!"

Stocks – "If you invest in a company you believe in, and it does well, your money grows too like being part of their success!"

Digital Gold – "It's like owning gold, but online! You don't have to keep it at home, and its value can increase over time."

Fixed Deposits (FDs) – "A super safe way to save! The bank keeps your money and adds extra (interest) over time, helping it grow steadily."

Veer listening closely, said, "This sounds cool! But how do I start?

"For now, an FD is the best option for you," Sanvi said.

"You can explore the rest when you're older, but it's always great to start learning about these things early!"

"Alright! I'm going to start an FD and let my money level up before the next sale."

Sanvi gave him a high-five. "Now that's smart saving!"

Ayan felt excited, not just about gaming, but about the idea of winning with money.

That night, Ayan read about stocks and investments. He was fascinated by how people can buy shares in companies they believe in, and watch their value grow over the years. He learned that when a company does well, its stock price increases, and investors can make money by selling their shares at a higher price. Some companies even pay dividends- extra money just for holding their stocks!

Ayan thought, "So, if I invest in a company like my favourite gaming brand, I could actually earn money as they grow?" The idea of being even a small part-owner in a big company thrilled him.

The next day, he asked Sanvi, "How do people buy stocks?"

Sanvi smiled. "Great question! People buy stocks through something called a stock exchange, like the Bombay Stock Exchange in India. They use special apps or brokers to buy and sell shares. But before investing, they research the company, checking if it's doing well, how much profit it makes, and if it's likely to grow in the future."

"So, you have to be smart about where you put your money?" Ayan asked.

"Exactly!" Sanvi nodded. "In investing, you have to plan your moves and make smart choices based on information. Some people invest for a long time, letting their money grow over years. Others trade more often. But the most important thing is to learn and start small."

Ayan was impressed. "This is like a strategy game in real life! I'm going to read more and, maybe one day, I'll invest in a company."

Sanvi patted his back. "That's the spirit! The more you learn now, the better decisions you'll make in the future."

Ayan was convinced to start reading more and tell his friends what he had learned.

The stock of this Chennai-headquartered company has witnessed an impressive rise over the years. On October 17, 2001, its stock price was ₹401.00, and in recent years, it has surged past ₹1 lakh. Investors who held onto its shares from the early days have seen substantial returns, reflecting the company's steady growth. Known for signing numerous athletes, which company is this?

You have learned about investments and may have some ideas. If you could invest in any company product or idea real or imaginary what would it be and why?

Chapter 8
Taxes and the Role of Government

It was a breezy Saturday afternoon when Pia, Ayan, Veer, and Misha finally set off for the new café a few blocks from their homes. They had been eagerly waiting for this day, having saved up their pocket money for two weeks. The café was famous for its desserts, especially its Tres Leches, and they could not wait to try it.

At around 3 PM, as they made their way to the café, a light drizzle began. They quickened their pace, hoping to reach before it started pouring. Just as they were about to step inside, they spotted Veer's older cousins, Neel and Geet, walking towards the entrance.

"Are you guys here for their famous desserts too?" Neel asked, grinning.

Veer, excited to see them, nodded enthusiastically. "Yes! We've been hearing so much about their Tres Leches. We even planned this for weeks!"

Misha added dramatically, "I ate a tiny lunch just to make room for all the food!"

Pia and Ayan chuckled, agreeing that they had done the same.

Once inside, they were mesmerized by the delicious aroma of freshly baked pastries and brewed coffee. The menu had so many tempting options that they found it hard to decide. They even asked the server to return a couple of times before finally placing their order, one meal each, their favourite boba drinks, and four desserts to share.

Seated at the table next to them, Neel and Geet overheard their order. "Wow, you guys must be really hungry," Geet teased.

Veer laughed. "We've been planning this for so long! We're going to eat till we drop."

After an indulgent meal filled with laughter, they asked for the bill. As they started splitting the cost among themselves, something caught their attention.

"Wait, why is the bill so high?" Ayan frowned, examining the receipt closely. "Look at this! The GST is a lot, and there's a service charge too. Plus, they added packing charges, but we didn't even ask them to pack anything!"

The group was puzzled. They had budgeted carefully, but the unexpected charges had thrown off their calculations. They discussed the issue among themselves until Neel and Geet noticed their concern.

> In the 18th century, England introduced a tax on a specific household feature, charging homeowners based on its number to recover revenue lost due to coin clipping. For instance, in 1747, houses with 10 to 14 of these were taxed at 6 pennies per unit, increasing to 9 pennies for more. To avoid the tax, many homeowners bricked them up.
> **Which household feature was taxed?**
>
> ------------------------------

> When the GST Bill was announced on July 1, 2017, tax rates on items such as gold, textiles, footwear, and others were decided by the finance minister Arun Jaitley.
> However, three specific items that were strongly associated with the Indian Independence struggle, have been declared tax-free under the GST regime.
> **If Khadi yarn and Gandhi cap are 2 of these, which is the 3rd item?**
>
> ------------------------------

"What's going on?" Neel asked.

Pia held up the receipt. "This café is so expensive! The GST and service charge are really high. Why do they even tax so much? What's the need for it?"

Neel nodded knowingly. "This is normal in restaurants and cafés. Let me have a look."

Geet inspected the bill as well. "Did you guys ask them to pack anything?"

"No, we didn't," Ayan replied.

Neel suggested they inform the server about the mistake. They called the staff over, and soon, a corrected bill was issued without the unnecessary packing charges.

After settling the bill, the friends walked out, satisfied with their delicious meal but still curious about the taxes they had paid. Neel and Geet walked alongside them as they headed back to their neighbourhood.

Veer, still pondering over the bill, turned to Neel. "Neel bro, why do they add so much GST? If we've already paid for the food, shouldn't that be enough? I don't like this system."

Neel smiled, realizing this was an opportunity to explain something important. "I get why you feel that way, but taxes like GST aren't just random extra charges. The government collects taxes to fund things that benefit everyone like building roads, maintaining public transport, running schools, and even providing healthcare services. Every time you buy something, whether it's groceries, video games, or even movie tickets, you're paying a little bit towards the country's growth."

"Interesting...What are the types of taxes in India?", asked Ayan

Neel replied, "India has a structured tax system that includes direct and indirect taxes."

> **Did You KNOW?**
> Denmark introduced a cow tax to reduce carbon emissions and promote sustainable farming. This tax targets explicitly methane, a powerful greenhouse gas emitted by livestock, particularly cows. The goal is to encourage farmers to adopt eco-friendly practices.

QUESTION

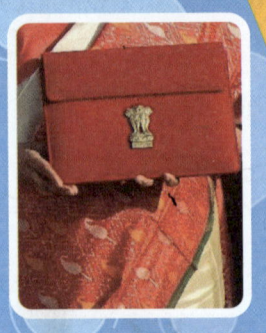

In 2019, Finance Minister gave up the British tradition of carrying a briefcase. She carried the budget documents in a four-fold red cloth (bahi-khata) with the national emblem on it.
In 2021, the traditional bahi khata was replaced due to the pandemic.
What was the bahi khata replaced with?

Elizabeth Magie, a game designer, writer, and feminist, was inspired by the ideas of economist Henry George. She advocated for a universal land tax based on a property's usefulness, size, and location rather than taxing income.
Her beliefs led her to create which board game, originally called The Landlord's Game?

"Let me break it down for you," Neel said. "Taxes are mainly of two types: Direct Taxes and Indirect Taxes."

Ayan looked curious. "What's the difference?"

Neel explained, "Direct Taxes are paid by individuals or businesses based on their income or profits. Let me break it down for you.
There is Income Tax – If someone earns money through a salary or business profits, they have to pay a portion of it as tax.
Corporate Tax – Big companies also pay taxes on the money they make.
Capital Gains Tax – When people sell property, shares, or gold and make a profit, they pay a tax on that profit."

Ayan nodded. "Okay, so that's money people or companies pay directly. What about Indirect Taxes?"

"Good question!" Neel continued. "Indirect Taxes are paid when we buy things. They're already included in the price. There is the Goods and Services Tax (GST). Note that in almost everything we buy has GST added to its price. Expensive things like luxury cars and watches have higher GST, while essential goods like vegetables and medicines have lower GST."

Neel paused and said, "So, let me tell you about two taxes.
Customs Duty – When products are brought from other countries, an extra tax is added to their price.
Stamp Duty – When buying property or land, people pay a tax to legally register it."

While this north-eastern Indian state may be small, it has zero income tax. Its tax policy has the potential to attract high-net-worth individuals and businesses. It became part of India in 1975. Which state is it?

Ayan's eyes lit up with understanding. "So, taxes help the government collect money to improve the country?"

"Exactly!" Neel said.

Geet, who was agreeing to what Neel, added, "For thousands of years, governments have used taxes to fund projects, maintain armies, and provide public services. Taxation dates to ancient times, with civilizations such as Mesopotamia, Egypt, Greece, and Rome implementing their own systems. Instead of money, early taxes were often collected in the form of goods, labour, or crops."

Neel added, "Think about it this way, imagine if there were no taxes. Who would build new highways, repair streetlights, or make sure we have clean water? The government uses these taxes to improve the country."

Geet agreed and said, "Exactly. In ancient Egypt, farmers contributed a share of their harvest as tax, while in ancient Rome, citizens paid in coins, goods, or even military service."

> In 1698, Tsar Peter I, also known as Peter the Great, introduced a tax to encourage Russians to adopt European. However, this tax was not met well by the public as it was a means of keeping a certain part of the body warm during harsh winters.
> **What did he tax?**
>
> ----------------------------------

Ayan's eyes sparkled with understanding. "Oh, so the government collects money to make the country better?"

"That's right!" Neel replied. "And not everything is taxed the same way. Expensive items like luxury cars or jewellery have higher taxes, while necessities like fresh vegetables and medicines have lower taxes
Misha sighed dramatically, "Okay, fine... but I still wish desserts were tax-free!"

Everyone laughed as they continued their walk home, now with full stomachs and a better understanding of why taxes exist.

> Introduced in 1860 by British finance minister James Wilson to address the financial crisis post-1857 rebellion, this tax became a key part of India's economy. After independence in 1947, an Act passed in 1961 continues to serve as its foundation. This tax is imposed on individuals and businesses based on their earnings?
> **Which tax is it?**
>
> ----------------------------------

Quest

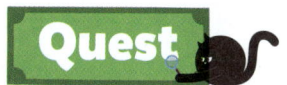

Imagine you were in charge of collecting taxes in your country. What would you tax more or less, and how would you use the funds to improve life for everyone?

Chapter 9
Understanding Debt and Borrowing

It was the last week of summer break, and Ayan and his friends were determined to make the most of it. The day before, Pia had suggested they do something fun, and Veer excitedly told them that his older cousin, Neel, was planning a trip to WonderLa Amusement Park, especially to try out the new cold-water rides.

The four friends were thrilled and immediately called Neel to ask if they could join.

"Of course! The more, the merrier! But we'll need to book the tickets soon," Neel replied.

Veer, Ayan, Pia, and Misha were all in! They eagerly waited for the ticket prices and other details. A few minutes later, Neel sent them a message with the total cost, including entry tickets and food expenses. Everyone had been saving up their pocket money for fun activities, but as Misha checked her wallet, her heart sank.

Founded in 1472, this is the world's oldest bank still in operation. Originally a pawn agency to support the underprivileged, it evolved into a leading financial institution. Today, it has 1,252 branches and operates in countries like India, Morocco, China, Tunisia, and Russia.
It is based in the country with the most UNESCO World Heritage Sites. Which country is it?

"Oh no! I don't have enough money," she muttered. She really didn't want to miss out, especially since she hadn't visited the park since its major upgrade.

She thought for a moment and then ran to her older brother.

"Hey, I need a small favour," Misha said sweetly.

Her brother raised an eyebrow. "What now?"

"So... my friends and I are going to Wonderla, and summer break is almost over... You get the point, right?" she said, trying to give her best puppy-dog eyes.

"Okay, so go. Why are you telling me this?" he asked, smirking.

Misha sighed dramatically. "Well, I might need to borrow some money."

Her brother laughed. "You always do this! You should really start saving from your allowance, Misha. But fine, I'll lend you the money... but on one condition."

Misha's face lit up. "Anything!"

"You have to return it with a little extra as interest," he said, grinning.

Misha looked confused. "What? What's interest?"

Her brother leaned back and explained, "Interest is the extra amount you pay when you borrow money. It's like a small fee for borrowing. Banks do the same thing when they lend money. But don't worry, I was just kidding. I won't charge you interest!"

Misha, now curious, asked, "Wait, how does borrowing and interest actually work?"

Her brother thought for a moment and then explained, "Right now, you don't have enough money for the amusement park, so you're borrowing from me and promising to return it later. That's exactly how a bank works! People borrow money from banks for big things like buying a house, starting a business, or even paying for college. This borrowed money is called a loan."

"Okay... and the interest part?" Misha asked.

"Good question! When you take a loan from a bank, you have to pay back more than you borrowed. The extra amount is called interest. That's how banks make money," her brother explained.

He continued, "For example, if you borrow ₹5,000 from a bank, they might say, 'You must return ₹5,000 plus ₹500 as interest.' So, you'll end up paying ₹5,500 in total. And here's the catch, if you take a long time to repay, the interest keeps adding up, and you owe even more!"

The word "bank" originates from the Italian word "banca," which means bench. In medieval Italy, moneylenders carried out business on benches in town markets.

Misha frowned. "That doesn't seem fair. If I borrowed ₹5,000, why can't I just return ₹5,000?"

Her brother replied, "Because banks also need to make money! They use interest to pay their employees, lend more money to others and keep customers' savings safe"

Misha nodded. "Okay, that makes sense. But what happens if someone doesn't pay the bank back?"

> The International Finance Corporation named the Indian rupee bonds issued in offshore capital markets. This name is inspired by a well-known Indian spice and reflects India's culture and cuisine. What is it?
>
> ---------------

The day of the trip finally arrived! The group was buzzing with excitement as they discussed the thrilling rides they wanted to try first. While waiting in line for the roller coaster, Misha told them about borrowing money from her brother and what she had learned about interest.

"Wait, so banks actually charge extra money when you borrow? That doesn't seem fair!" Pia said.

Neel shook his head. "But that's how banks work. If they didn't charge interest, how would they make money? If they only gave out money without getting anything in return, banks wouldn't last very long!"

> **Did You KNOW?**
>
> There are different types of educational loans:
> Domestic Education Loans: For pursuing studies within the country.
> Overseas Education Loans: For those enrolling in educational programs abroad.
> Skill Development Loans: For short-term courses or vocational training programs.

"What are the eligibility criteria to get an education loan?" asked Pia.

Neel answered, "Good question. Let me put it in points.
• The applicant must be an Indian citizen with confirmed admission to a recognized institution.
• A co-applicant, such as a parent or guardian, is often required.
• Collateral may be necessary for higher loan amounts, depending on the bank's policy."

Neel continued, "Loans can be really helpful if used wisely. There are even different types of loans, like education loans, home loans, and car loans. Some people even mortgage their property to get a loan."

Misha raised an eyebrow. "Mortgage? What's that?"

"It means offering something valuable, like your house or gold, as security. If you can't pay back the loan, the bank takes that property instead," Neel explained.

Veer looked surprised. "Wow! So what are the different types of loans?"

Neel smiled. "Good question! There are two main types, secured and unsecured loans.
Secured Loans require you to pledge a valuable asset, such as property or gold, as security. Common examples include home loans, gold loans, and car loans.
Unsecured Loans have no collateral required, but they typically come with higher interest rates. Examples include personal loans, education loans, and business loans.
Other Types of Loans like agricultural loans and microfinance loans are designed to support farmers and small businesses.

Misha said, "This is actually interesting! Who knew a simple trip to an amusement park would turn into a finance lesson?"

Neel laughed. "Well, now you know how important borrowing wisely is!"

As they boarded their next ride, Misha thought to herself, Maybe I should start saving more... so I don't have to borrow next time.

The Creditio Emiliano Bank, also known as Credem is a bank in Reggio Emilia, Italy.
They are known to accept an unusual item as collateral for loans which serves as a valuable collateral for the bank.
What item is used as collateral?

This is the currency Rupiah. The name "Rupiah" is derived from the Sanskrit word for silver, 'Rupyakam'. Sometimes, the locals of the country also informally use the word "perak" referring to rupiah in coins.
Which country's currency is this that features a Ganesha?

If a bank mistakenly added extra money into your account, would you consider it "borrowing" if you used it? Why or why not?

Chapter 10
Future Financial Goals

The summer break had come to an end, and Ayan, Pia, Veer, and Misha felt they had made the most of their time at home. As they walked towards the bus stop on the first day of school, their conversation drifted towards something they had been thinking about setting financial goals.

"Have you decided on your financial goal, Misha?" Ayan asked as they walked along the familiar road, the morning sun casting long shadows on the pavement.

Misha's eyes lit up. "Yes, Ayan! I've been thinking about setting a small goal, nothing too big, just something practical and important for me."

"And what is that?" Ayan asked, curious.

Before Misha could answer, Veer came running towards them, slightly out of breath. He held up a crumpled sheet of paper, his face beaming with excitement.

"Look at this!" Veer panted, waving the paper in front of them. "I found this cool website that gives tips on how to plan for future financial goals. I wrote down some ideas!"

"That's great, Veer," Ayan said, taking a glance at the notes. "Pia and I were just talking about this. Pia was about to share her plan."

> On March 2009, the government announced a contest to design something Indian in nature.
> There were about 3300 contestants out of which an IIT professor D Udaya Kumar's submission was selected. This was then used to represent something which we all use.
>
> **What did Udaya Kumar design?**
>
> ---------------------------------

Pia smiled, her eyes twinkling with excitement. "So, my family and I are planning a trip to Europe during the Dussehra holidays, super exciting, right? But, wow, planning a trip is incredibly expensive! I've been watching my parents' budget for flights, hotels, and everything, and it got me thinking... what if I saved up some money before then?"

Veer raised an eyebrow. "Wait, wait, wait... are you saying you're saving up for a shopping spree in Paris?"

Pia laughed. "Well, maybe a tiny one! But more than that, I want to be able to buy a few things for myself without constantly asking my parents for extra cash. And if I save enough, who knows? Maybe I'll even surprise them with a nice dinner one night!"

Ayan chimed in. "Whoa, look at you, Miss Independent! A fancy dinner in Europe? That's next-level!"

Misha nudged her playfully. "Let's hope you don't end up with just enough to buy one dessert!"

Everyone laughed as Pia rolled her eyes. "Well, that's why I need a solid savings plan! No desserts-only dinners for me!"

She continued, "I also learned about some fascinating schemes in our country, things I would have completely missed if we weren't on this journey of financial literacy!"

Ayan added, "Oh yes! My cousin's friend volunteered at a school in a rural area, and she told me that students there receive free meals to improve nutrition and encourage attendance. She said it was an amazing experience!"

This Government-sponsored scheme allows individuals to invest in low-risk equity funds for good returns, offers tax benefits, and provides flexibility in fund allocation.
It's a smart way to save for retirement while securing for future.
Which scheme is this?

A national initiative, launched in 2015, aims to address the declining child sex ratio and is jointly run by the Ministries of Women & Child Development, Health & Family Welfare, and Education. It primarily focuses on regions in Uttar Pradesh, Haryana, Uttarakhand, Punjab, Bihar, and Delhi.
Name the scheme.

"Your Europe trip saving plan sounds exciting, Pia!" Misha said. "I was thinking of something similar but on a smaller scale. I want to save up for a good bicycle. I could use it to get to school and tuition classes instead of relying on public transport all the time. If I start saving a little each month, I think I can reach my goal in a year!"

Ayan nodded thoughtfully. "That's a great idea, Misha! My plan is a bit different. I want to start investing small amounts. Maybe I'll ask my dad to do that for me; it is just good to know even small savings can grow over time. I thought it would be cool to learn about investments early."

"That sounds interesting!" Pia said. "I never really thought about investing before, but it does sound like a good way to grow money over time. Maybe I should look into it, too."

Veer grinned. "Wow, we all have such different goals! I was thinking of saving up for a trip. I love traveling, and I thought it would be fun to plan and save for my own trip instead of always depending on my parents."

Pia nodded. "That's amazing, Veer! It's so cool how we're all thinking ahead in different ways. Maybe we can help each other stay on track."

"Good idea!" Veer said. "How about we create a financial goal journal and update it every month? We can keep track of our progress and share tips along the way."

"That sounds like a plan," Ayan said. "And if we ever get stuck, we can do research together or ask adults for advice."

As they reached the bus stop, the group felt more excited than ever, not just about school but about the possibilities that lay ahead. They knew that setting goals was just the first step, but with the right mindset, a little discipline, and the support of their friends, they could achieve anything.

QUESTION

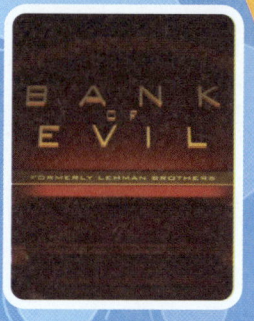

'The Bank of Evil' is a fictional financial institution that appears in an animated film series. This bank is a reference to Lehman Brothers, an investment bank that collapsed in 2008.
Which film series features this bank?

One of the earliest examples of an economic collapse was in the Netherlands. Prices of the flower pictured ballooned until a sudden crash in 1637.
Which flower inspired this mania?

If you were given ₹10,000 today to start working towards a future financial goal, what would you do with it?

The best route your  story can take.

To publish your own book, contact us.

We publish poetry collections, short story collections, novellas and novels.

IndiePress

contact@http://indiepress.in/

Instagram-indie_press